DANGEROUS JOURNEYS

EXPLORING MOUNT EVEREST

BY BETSY RATHBURN

BELLWETHER MEDIA · MINNEAPOLIS, MN

TM

Torque brims with excitement
perfect for thrill-seekers of all kinds.
Discover daring survival skills, explore
uncharted worlds, and marvel at mighty
engines and extreme sports. In *Torque* books,
anything can happen. Are you ready?

This edition first published in 2023 by Bellwether Media, Inc.

No part of this publication may be reproduced in whole or in part without
written permission of the publisher. For information regarding permission,
write to Bellwether Media, Inc., Attention: Permissions Department,
6012 Blue Circle Drive, Minnetonka, MN 55343.

Library of Congress Cataloging-in-Publication Data

LC record for Exploring Mount Everest available at:
https://lccn.loc.gov/2022012976

Text copyright © 2023 by Bellwether Media, Inc. TORQUE and associated
logos are trademarks and/or registered trademarks of Bellwether Media, Inc.

Editor: Kieran Downs   Designer: Josh Brink

Printed in the United States of America, North Mankato, MN.

TABLE OF CONTENTS

BASE CAMP

After days of hiking, the climbers have finally reached the foot of the mountain. Snowy **peaks** rise around them. They are at a Mount Everest **base camp**!

The climbers set up their tents. Now they must rest and get used to the conditions. Soon, they will climb to the **summit**!

BASE CAMP

WAY TO M.T. EVEREST B.C.

TWO WAYS UP

THE SOUTH COL AND THE
NORTHEAST RIDGE ARE THE TWO
MAIN PATHS UP MOUNT EVEREST.
THE SOUTH COL ROUTE IS THE
MOST POPULAR.

WORLD'S TALLEST

MOUNT EVEREST

Mount Everest is the world's tallest mountain. It lies between Nepal and China. It rises more than 29,000 feet (8,839 meters) above sea level!

April and May make up the mountain's busiest climbing season. Some climbers also visit in September, October, and November. It takes around 10 weeks to make the climb to the top.

MOUNT EVEREST MAP

MOUNT EVEREST = ◇   NEPAL = ◆

CHINA = ◆

Many people have tried to climb Mount Everest. The first successful attempt was recorded in 1953. Edmund Hillary and Tenzing Norgay reached the top! Since then, thousands of people have reached the summit. Many people who climb Everest are **mountaineers**. They climb for fun. Scientists may climb to study **climate change** or plant life.

EDMUND HILLARY

TENZING NORGAY

MOUNTAINEER

NOTABLE EXPLORER

NAME: KAMI RITA

BORN: JANUARY 17, 1970

JOURNEY: ATTEMPTED TO REACH THE SUMMIT FOR HIS 25TH TIME IN MAY 2021

RESULTS: BROKE HIS OWN WORLD RECORD FOR MOST SUCCESSFUL MOUNT EVEREST CLIMBS

PLANNING AND PREPARATION

Mount Everest explorers must be fit and healthy. Many train by carrying heavy packs up and down hills. It can take a year or more to train properly.

Climbers should also be experienced. Many climb other tall mountains to prepare. They learn how to use climbing tools. They know how to survive dangerous mountain weather.

SHERPAS

Many climbers plan their trips with **expedition companies**. These companies help climbers get **permits**. They offer guides. They also work with **Sherpas** who help set up routes and carry supplies.

Climbing Mount Everest is expensive. Some trips cost over $100,000! Climbers often try to find **sponsors**. Governments or companies pay for the trip!

PLANNING YOUR JOURNEY

EXERCISE REGULARLY

PRACTICE CLIMBING DIFFICULT MOUNTAINS

PLAN WITH AN EXPEDITION COMPANY

GET A PERMIT AND PAY FEES

ON TOP OF THE WORLD

Mount Everest journeys start before base camp. Climbers hike for around two weeks to reach the camp. Then, they stay at base camp for another four weeks. This helps avoid **altitude sickness**. Climbers at base camp watch the weather carefully. Good weather means they can start their climb.

FREEZING COLD

THE TEMPERATURE NEAR THE PEAK NEVER RISES ABOVE FREEZING. CLIMBERS MUST BE CAREFUL TO KEEP CLOTHING WARM AND DRY.

WHAT HAPPENS WHEN YOU GET ALTITUDE SICKNES?

DIZZINESS

HEADACHE

SHORTNESS OF BREATH

UNABLE TO WALK OR MOVE

Climbers face many dangers. Giant **seracs** rise along the Khumbu Icefall. These ice towers can fall and block paths. They can also hit climbers!

SERAC

WATCH YOUR STEP!

THE KHUMBU ICEFALL MOVES! SUNSHINE MELTS THE ICE AND MAKES IT SHIFT. THIS MAKES THE AREA ONE OF THE MOST DANGEROUS PARTS OF THE JOURNEY.

CREVASSE

CRAMPON

Deep **crevasses** are also dangerous. People can fall into them and get trapped. Climbers wear **crampons** to hold onto the ice. They tie themselves to ropes along the route to avoid falling.

AVALANCHE

Avalanches can wipe out climbing paths or bury climbers. Climbers must know where avalanches can happen. They must look for signs.

DEATH ZONE

WHEN CLIMBERS REACH 26,247 FEET (8,000 METERS), THEY HAVE ENTERED MOUNT EVEREST'S DEATH ZONE. PEOPLE WITHOUT BOTTLED OXYGEN CANNOT SURVIVE IN THIS AREA FOR LONG.

OXYGEN MASK

It is hard to breathe at high altitudes. Climbers rely on bottled **oxygen** as they climb above base camp. They reach the final camp after a week!

From the final camp, climbers start towards the peak. After about 10 hours of climbing, they arrive at the summit! They take pictures and enjoy the view.

But they cannot stay long. They must climb down before dark. Those who make it have completed one of the world's most dangerous journeys. They have reached the top of the world!

GLOSSARY

altitude sickness—a serious illness caused when people go to high-altitude areas; altitude refers to how high a place is above sea level.

avalanches—masses of snow, ice, and rocks that fall down mountains

base camp—a campsite near the summit of Mount Everest where climbers rest and get ready to climb

climate change—a human-caused change in Earth's weather due to warming temperatures

crampons—pieces of metal with sharp spikes that attach to shoes or boots to help climbers stand on ice

crevasses—deep cracks

expedition companies—companies that help people plan big trips; expeditions are trips taken with a particular purpose.

mountaineers—people who take part in the sport of climbing mountains

oxygen—a gas needed to breathe

peaks—the tops of mountains

permits—official papers that show people are allowed to do or have something

seracs—tall blocks of ice on glaciers or mountains

Sherpas—people who live in the Himalayan region of Nepal and China; Sherpas often serve as guides on mountain-climbing trips.

sponsors—governments, businesses, or individuals that provide money to do something

summit—the highest point of a mountain

TO LEARN MORE

AT THE LIBRARY

London, Martha. *Mount Everest.* Minneapolis, Minn.: Abdo Publishing, 2021.

Stewart, Alexandra. *Everest: The Remarkable Story of Edmund Hillary and Tenzing Norgay.* New York, N.Y.: Bloomsbury, 2020.

Tolli, Jenna. *The Highest Peak: How Mount Everest Formed.* New York, N.Y.: PowerKids Press, 2020.

ON THE WEB

FACTSURFER

Factsurfer.com gives you a safe, fun way to find more information.

1. Go to www.factsurfer.com

2. Enter "exploring Mount Everest" into the search box and click Q.

3. Select your book cover to see a list of related content.

INDEX

The images in this book are reproduced through the courtesy of: Travel_Photoshoot, front cover (hero); Vixit, front cover (Mount Everest), pp. 3, 13 (climbing), 21; Daniel Prudek, pp. 4, 5 (all); Zzvet, p. 6; Keystone-France/ Getty Images, p. 8; Alun Richardson/ Alamy, pp. 9, 17, 19; NAVESH CHITRAKAR/ Alamy, p. 9 (Kami Rita); lzf, p. 10; Inu, p. 11; Timur Bizhigitov, pp. 12-13; Maridav, p. 13 (exercise); 135pixels, p. 13 (expedition company); RomanR, p. 13 (permit); CI2/ Alamy, p. 14; Leremy, p. 15; Kenneth Koh/ Adventure Nomad/ Getty Images, p. 16; 24K-Production, p. 17 (crampon); RafalBelzowski/ Getty Images, p. 18; VCG/ Contributor/ Getty Images, p. 20.